25 Poems of the Heart

RENEE' ANDERSON

Copyright © 2018 Renee' Anderson

All rights reserved. No part of this publication may be reproduced, distributed, or transmitted in any form or by any means, including photocopying, recording, or other electronic or mechanical methods, without the prior written permission of the publisher, except in the case of brief quotations embodied in critical reviews and certain other noncommercial uses permitted by copyright law.

ISBN-13: 978-1-945532-98-6

Library of Congress Number:

Published by Opportune Independent Publishing Company

For permission requests, write to the publisher, addressed "Attention: Permissions Coordinator" to the address below.

Email: Info@opportunepublishing.com

Address: 113 N. Live Oak Street
　　　　　Houston, TX 77003

This book is dedicated to the generation from my womb; nothing is impossible with God.

—Luke 1:37

25 Poems of the Heart

Missing You

Gentle words that blend with the wind
Softly brushed against my ear
Warm firm compassionate hands
Respectfully they grasp
Beautiful brown eyes that reveal the soul
A convincing smile
Patient
A gentlemen's style
Cavity sweet
Intune with the Creator
Grounded, relaxed
Never meeting a stranger
Protecting what is loved
Cautious of what is near
Searching for the right one
Careful not to prematurely give
A glow upon his satin skin
It mirrors his purpose within
Never have written words been so true
I, miss, you

(Only love can do that) I will

When you frustrate me, I am patient
Only love can do that
When you offend me, understanding embraces me like a thread of soft silk pearls
Only love can do that
When you say things that anger me, forgiveness is my crown
When I'm disappointed and feeling hurt, suddenly I remember why I fell in love with you and it wipes away every record
Only love can do that
When you leave my side, though it's only for a moment,
Kind words and a gently touch is eagerly waiting for your return
Only love can do that
When life presents a greater challenge, making it easy to throw in the towel
I'll pray for you
I'll encourage you
I'll have faith for you
Day after day
Hour after hour
Only love can do that
When you are successful and accomplishing great things
Gladness will be my shoes as I run and sing God's praises on the roof top
No pride or competition here; just gratefulness from the bottom of

           my heart
      Only love can do that.

Knowing

When you feel in a deep place with no words to describe

A pull, a draw, a knowing inside

An aching

Restlessness

A groaning from within

Curiosity mostly

It's hard to pretend

Days go by, not one word spoken

Even in the silence my feelings continue to grow

Secure, confident

Certain if he's near curious eyes will definitely know

Weeks go by and now it's been months

Each glimpse of you helps me to hold on

It is not a dream

It is a never-ending love

Stringing me along desperately hoping what I know is not wrong

Free

In another space

Without guilt or shame

Above the eyes that judge and blame

Hidden from the vile that thrust from their lips

Light

Floating in peace

So protected by Him

I'm impossible to reach

The unbearable memories are gone

That tortured me

Almost destroyed me

As the tears flowed like a long hopeless song

No longer a beast

Commanded here and there to please

I can dance and escape

Hidden in His shadows

Covered by His wings

Newness kissed my face

Love laid hold of my chest

And as I take each breath

Forgiveness draws me out

Suspending me far above time and space

With no reason or rhyme

This freedom is mine to keep

Overshadowed by the new me melody

No limits in this direction

Joy embraced me and won all my affection

Faithful eyes seeing success

A mind complex in its process

Organizing all the information

Putting every question to rest

My center being resist gravity

Legs that run to prove

As long as I'm in you

I could never be removed from this place called free

His Eyes

They tell a story we often hear

About pain, disappointment, and sometimes despair

They tell a story that's clear to me

Of a journey no man should have to travel

A betrayal no one should ever feel

This man you see, has a few things missing

Loyalty, trust, unconditional love; holy matrimony

Eyes misguided, unfaithful, determined to retaliate

A woman's touch created this

Replacing love with hate

Yes his eyes tell many stories and they are all clear to me

Healing, restoration

A whole heart is yours to keep

Love without fear or hesitation

A new experience awaits

God intended happiness to be your destination

One day his eyes will tell a new story

The beginning of something great

How he's overcome the sadness

How he took back his victory

His eyes will tell you about a new man

This journey was all a part of the plan

The Separation

No voice to speak

No strength to stand

My fight is gone

I accept my wrong

Defeat is standing on my chest

He's bigger than me

It's hard to rest

The end was quick

It passed right by

11 years felt like an entire lifetime

Damaged tissue everywhere

Hearts shredded into pieces

Hope stolen by shame

Not sure where to place the blame

No voice to speak

No strength to stand

Fear has me arrested, chained and bound by gag

Confusion slit my wrist

My love bleeds to the floor

Spinning in circles

It's hard to ignore

I turn my face to you

But the emptiness grows more and more

No voice to speak

No strength to stand

There was nothing to compare

Seemed like my last chance

To live

To love

Punished for taking a stand

So what I recommend

Let hurt have free range

An expiration date has been set

No voice to speak in this season of silence

The moment is gone

There's no point in trying

No strength to stand for this time of rest

It is greatly needed

I must recuperate

Be fully equipped

To overcome the next big test

Comfortable Me

I'm comfortable being me
Dancing free and carelessly
Laughing as I socialize
A nurturing caregiver to my surprise
Ambitious ready to succeed
Standing strong in who I believe
What I believe
Comfortable, being me

Always striving to do my best
Satisfied, though perhaps not accepted by the rest
Juggling many gifts deep inside
Cold stairs, sleepless nights,
Hungry all the time
To humble and grateful to carry pride

Hurt at times, even filled with despair
Determined to break the generational curse
Forgiveness I must bear
Wounded relationships once
Were smiling faces

As I erase the old them

A few accomplishments
Their value is slim to none
Graduation, marriage, children
Relationships all rolled in one
Become the size of a flea
If I'm not comfortable being me

So I encourage you
To join me as I appreciate
He who created you and me
Relax and be yourself
As I am comfortable being me

Love

Reduce to little or no value

Manipulated for personal gain

Repetitious in use, yet she still has hope

Perhaps it's just easier for her to hide

Decorated beautifully at times

Second best to the sensual desires

Few exists that still believe in her

Her strength is a hidden truth

The invaluable glue

She's happy to pierce their hearts

Enamored as she motivates them to sing

Her burrowed roots draw insomnia in the dark

The warmth of her peace makes it easy to yield

The kindness of her fingertips drive out the deepest fears

Her patience secure a timeless bond

Provoking loyalty no matter the circumstance

She is coveted by many but reside with the brave

And no matter where she goes or where she is

Her faith is strong, believing, there is another chance.

The Heart

It's the constant beat

As the ocean is deep

Perplexed emotions creep

Some lows some highs

Waves rise and tides ride

Into the oceans sand

Let love begin

Don't want the same

Disappointment and hurt again

It's a surf board

Blend in until you see that high wave come in

Valves pump and keep stability

Unashamed of the loyal part of me

As blood of the heart flows

People come and people go

They cause the heart to know

Not one day is promised

Every moment is counted

The heart doesn't think

It instinctively beats

Fearless indeed

Veins that wrap around completely

Holding you close as you feel me beating

Letting Go

It's hard to laugh
Easy to cry
A bruised heart
Too many lies
The breaking of soul ties

Insecure faces
Broken in several places
Exhausted every option
Trusting is a problem

Flooded with chances
Too late to make plans and
Now it's confusing
When there is a lack of respect
It usually turns abusive

A dream is just a dream
Hope becomes smoke
And even though love still heals
Its absence is clear

Maturity is great

Two hearts bonded together is hard to break

Physically letting go is easy

The mind justifies the actions to appease me

Though it has been so long

The mind contemplates and the heart stays true

Refusing to let go of you

Love Dismantled Me

Unbothered by the walls of shame

Like a thief looking for spoils to gain

Love stole a place

Stared me right in the face but

Boldly I welcome the fight

Yet quieted as I was enlightened

Love had nothing to prove

It caught me

Hung me upside down

Didn't care if I disapproved

Mistrust surrounded me like barbed wire

Unflattered by words or things to be desired

Fueled by hurt

Self-Inspired

Filled with determination

But love never underestimated me

Tripped with feelings

Slammed on my back

Love penetrated me slowly

Held my mouth shut pinned my arms back

Impregnated me with anomalies

Lack of sleep

Hunger pains that run deep

Angry when I don't feel you near me

Jealousy

Driven by passion

Armed myself with bows and arrows

Grabbing hold as captain

Deceived by what happens next

Love comforted me

Wrapped my tightly and whispered, "trust me"

Its venom paralyzing

Falling so deep

Drowning as Love Dismantles Me

Believe

When those that are close

Dig up the past to justify why they wont support

When positivity has no relevancy in those who choose not to achieve

Still believe

When the incapacity to digest being oppressed refuses to lessen

Never digress

Its best when confidence is ceiling high

And fear is beneath too cold to even creep

Still believe

Its when we put away pride

Let the stones that build a wall of tenacity

Be the drive

Perpetual thoughts of suicide

Eating away at your soul at times

And deliverance seems a far reach

Still believe

When grief slips and bitterness sets in

When injustice stains the bed of trust

A bed of lies as evil and darkness filled the peoples eyes

Still Believe

As your Faith is challenged

While your life is in the balance

Hold on to your plea

Know your deliverance is coming

And never stop believing

Caused by the Wind

A breeze beneath my wing

Sun-kissed skin glowing

Set up to win

A new start

A fresh look

Above the clouds is where it all begins

Blinded with passion

Pregnant with love

For every loss there was twice the win

It propelled my wings to soar again

I've shedded the old

Refused to sell my soul

And because my life has purpose

My Spirit will never grow old

25 Poems of the Heart

Love Thoughts

Do you think of me as often as I think of you?

A mind that wonders

What it would be like

Reciprocating immense love for one another

Is your stomach in knots?

Over active sweat glands that won't stop

Bonded and understood

Locked down like Fort Knox

Does it make you uncomfortable?

A love this solid

Planted so deep without it feels hollow

Are you pressed between loving me and leaving?

Peeling away fear as we proceed to believe

We've build a love outside of the sheets

Two hearts that drum to the tune, I need you

Prepared to go through

Leaning desperately

Our paths crossed

Woven together intricately

Weighted down emotionally

Should this love be the anchor that keeps us closely?

Secure in every word

Trusting each action

Is there a love dressed in this fashion?

Both driven with passion

We still vibe through negative interactions

Is our love unique?

Individually complete

Yet when we're together our love flows naturally

Do you think of me as often as I think of you?

I'll hold you close

Never letting go

As only our love would do

The Many Colors of Me

Recklessly searching here and there

I know who I am but no one else seems to care

They say I'm too bold

But it's two fold

When they need someone to speak

My voice is whom they seek

Ashamed

Embarrassed

Exposed with no mercy

They laugh

Even reject me

It doesn't matter how much they hurt me

It doesn't change who I am

Estrogen strong and doing all that I can

Gifted and equipped

When God thrust me forward I know He won't miss

Sometimes pulled back only to gain momentum

As the rock in a sling shot

I'm purposed without fail to be viewed by all of them

Recklessly searching here and there

I'm created to be who I am

No matter who does or does not care

25 Poems of the Heart

Pressing

Love with true love

Be angry but for a moment

Laugh from your soul

Live intentionally until you're old

Hold a friend with two hands

Look your enemies in the eyes

Create a plan for your dreams

Its rewarding to be kind to people that are mean

25 Poems of the Heart

The Games People Play

What is this thing we feel?

Why do we do the things we do?

How can we say what we say?

Are you sure we feel the same way?

We talk

We walk

We curl up on the side

Content and happy are the words we use to describe

What should we do?

Is it me or is it you?

Where do we go from here?

We like each other; so it appears

Maybe I'll go

Maybe I'll stay

Perplexed and undecided

Should we proceed with caution?

Not sure if we should go too deep

Too much emotion could cause an explosion

Too little in between could make anyone be mean

Why do we play the games we play?

Maybe I'll go

Maybe I'll stay

Three is enough or is it too much

It's fitting for a king; is this order too rough?

A past that makes him run for cover

Drama here and there; is there really another?

Fear is a thick cloud

Blinding us from what could be

Why do we play the games we play?

Because of fear of the unknown if we dare to stay

A Mothers Bond

More than the days we embraced

Deeper than the sense of your pain

Wider than the happiness from goals obtained

Through many laughs

Lost paths

Identity crisis

Discovering what this life is

Grateful for your life

Nothing should be changed

There was purpose in each exchange

Every memory big or small

Gods greatness in you

Removes the fear of it all

And no matter what each day brings

Regardless of the outcome

Nothing can replace our timeless bond

25 Poems of the Heart

Falling Short

Why was I judged

Why was I considered a waste

How come the purity in my words though they spoke truth

Didn't resonate with the integrity inside of you

Why was my faith too much

And my dreams to overcome mistrust in people not enough

The ability to cope with brokenness

Has made what was suppose to be a simple path

Into an abyss if deeply darkened sadness

And though what happened next is uncertain

Thoughts of picking up the pieces from the

Disappointment is a definite misfortune

25 Poems of the Heart

Confused hope

Two minds that wonder

Hearts that conquer

Places of discomfort from the coldness of departure

Secure but not sure

Mixed lust with trust

Emotions intertwined

Anger with heartache

A confused mind will let go

But your gravity doesn't hesitate

To hold me close

Many partners attached and revealed in time

Release my soul from their hold

Free my life from their grasp

Pieces of your life in their hands

And even though we cant seem to find our way

We both hold on to what is true

Waiting to be rescued

25 Poems of the Heart

Present Contentment

Beautiful are your eyes that gleam with gladness
A warm smile that melts the coldest hearts
Tender is your touch and
As the gossamer is carried away by a gentle breeze
So is the gentle flow of your kindness that reaches

Many receive you when you are near
Your generous embrace
Make your intentions clear
The kindness of your words
Becomes stable, remaining undisturbed

A smooth glide in your confident stride
A mind unbothered when tried at times
In the heart is where happiness reigns
Dwelling in your chest lies the bravery to love again

25 Poems of the Heart

Passionate Kisses

Each moment of your soft touch
Makes the chemistry grow
Feeling all of what you give
So intense it starts to show

Pressing against me here and there
The excitement is hard to bare
A sweet bliss to my surprise
I crave them all over my body

Refusing to hide
Inside are butterflies
Each time you pull me close
Every time your lips touch mine

25 Poems of the Heart

Close

Legs intertwined

From hearts opened wide

Delicate emotions

Surrounded by devotion

Together is what we are

Inside my thighs

Forever in life

Side by side

The truth is we don't mind

Being present with hope

Determined to stay close

As two paths that grow

Overlapping our souls

Forever we embrace

Our close space

25 Poems of the Heart

Pour Into Me

Pour into me

As quiet as you please

From the strength of my coiled dark hair

To my brass stained feet

The melanin in my skin is where it all begins

While my nose can smell for miles

Eyes stretched wide

Wisdom is my prize

Arms built to perfection

My inheritance is my collection

Large thighs help me rise high

And every organ in me

Gives strength to the population

Increasing their abilities

Emulated by most but humility shows

Receiving all I can from far above

Pure from the Creators love

25 Poems of the Heart

A Beautiful Place

When laughter is on the rise and the tide is high

Filling the space

Where the trees blow and the sea shells show

Just above the sand that rolls

As my footprints follow the sultry path

Soon the waves rush and crash

While marine life passes with each glide

It's the fresh scent of a beautiful life

Where tanned skin is bare and free

In a peaceful fashion

So much fun in action

Wet sand between my toes

And as the birds soar

Then rest where its safe

No one can avoid this beautiful place

About the Author

Renee Anderson is a freelance Graphic Designer and a writer of romantic short stories in addition to writing poetry. She won her first writing contest at 8 years old and was inspired to continue her writing journey from there. She is an active Booksie member and also enjoys connecting with other writers on Instagram.

www.ingramcontent.com/pod-product-compliance
Lightning Source LLC
Chambersburg PA
CBHW052209110526
44591CB00012B/2136